On a Roll!

By Diane L. Umansky

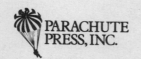

PARACHUTE
PRESS, INC.

Parachute Press, Inc.
156 Fifth Avenue
New York, New York 10010

First printing: March 1991
Printed in the U.S.A.

Design by Paul Matarazzo

COVER PHOTO CREDIT:
Courtesy of Rollerblade, Inc.

In-line skaters should observe all recommended safety precautions
described herein to reduce the risk of injury and are urged to seek the
advice of the national governing body for the sport of in-line skating.
Rollerblade In-Line Skate Association (RISA)

TABLE OF CONTENTS

BIG WHEELS, BIG DEAL!

1

Have you ever seen someone whizzing by on things that look like ski boots with neon-bright wheels? If so, you know what in-line skating looks like. This hot new sport is spreading across the country, and fast!

Experts in the roller skating industry think that about 600,000 people will buy a pair of in-line skates this year alone! And the leading maker of in-line skates, Rollerblade®, is quickly becoming a household name.

In-line skates are actually roller skates with the wheels lined up in one row instead of side by side. Because of the wheel position on the boot, in-line skates tend to go faster and turn more smoothly.

Kids are using their "in-lines" for all kinds of fun. Some love to glide along. Others work on learning radical tricks or speed skating. They can roll alone or

5

with friends—or play roller hockey or practice dance moves! And some kids use their skates for transportation—to school, to a friend's house, to parks and beaches.

In-line skating is definitely on a roll. Magazines such as *People, Seventeen, Health,* and *Life* have all reported on this popular new sport. Special roller-race clubs and roller hockey teams are springing up across the United States. And just last summer, a camp for in-line skaters opened up in California!

And kids aren't the only people who are enjoying the in-line craze. Messengers in big cities whirl through traffic on in-line skates to deliver packages. Store clerks at some large Price Savers stores even use in-lines to get around on the floor. Talk about quick service!

Top skaters have gotten so good on in-lines that they can flip, twirl, and spin on them. Some in-line skaters even use the ramps reserved for skateboarders! Team Rollerblade®, a group of professional skaters organized by Rollerblade, travel around the country and the world performing, teaching, and simply spreading the word. And believe it or not, the next Summer Olympic Games will have a roller skating exhibition that will also feature in-line skating!

To think that in-line skating started taking off only about ten years ago in Minnesota! At first it was just a way for ice hockey players to stay in shape off-season, and now it's keeping everybody in shape!

What do longtime skaters think about in-line skates? "It lets ice skaters use the world as their ice rink," says David Miles, president of the Outdoor Rollerskating Association of America (ORA). "It means freedom and excitement." And he should know. David Miles has been skating for twelve years and in-line skating since 1987!

So are you ready to get on a roll? Ready to get the scoop on in-line skates? Ready, set, let's roll!

AND THEN THERE WERE SKATES!

2

In-line skates seem to be the newest thing around, don't they? But did you know that this modern invention was created nearly 300 years ago? In-line skates were actually the very first skates!

The skating craze started in the early 1700s when an ice skater in Holland decided that he wanted to find a way to "ice skate" all year long. The Dutchman went to work making an "ice-skate" that he could use in warm weather. First he nailed wooden spools to pieces of wood. Then he nailed the pieces of wood in a row to the bottom of his shoes. And there they were: the world's first pair of in-line skates! The Dutchman thought his idea was exciting, but his invention never became a hit. Today, nobody even remembers his name!

But all was not lost. In 1760, a Belgian inventor and instrument maker named Joseph Merlin came up with his own version of the in-line skate. He was so proud of his invention that he decided to show off his metal-wheeled skates at a big masquerade ball! He made a dramatic entrance—rolling through the door while playing his violin.

But Mr. Merlin had forgotten one minor detail: he had not yet figured out how to stop his skates! So he crashed right into a huge mirror. Although his invention was a crashing failure, that didn't stop other people from working on new types of in-line roller skates.

Finally, in 1819, a Frenchman got a patent on a skate with copper, wood, or ivory wheels. The wheels were lined up in a row on the bottom of the skate. Unfortunately, his skate went in only one direction—forward.

After the 1819 skate, another man came up with the idea of a skate with five wheels in a row. This skate's biggest wheel was in the center and was used for turning. But even with this improvement, in-line skates remained difficult to use.

Then in 1849, the turning point came. A man by the name of Louis Legrange was asked to make skates for some actors in an opera. The composer wanted the actors to look as if they were ice skating. Legrange thought the women in the opera would have trouble skating on the in-line skates. He thought their ankles were too weak. So he made a special skate for the women. The skate had two pairs of wheels: one pair set side by side in the front of the skate and the other pair in the back. People paid attention to Legrange's invention. He had just invented the traditional roller skate.

Inventors in the United States got into the roller skating act in 1863. James Leonard Plimpton of Massachusetts created a roller skate that made turning easier. Like Legrange's skates, his had two pairs of wheels. But Plimpton placed one pair of wheels under the ball of the foot and the other under the heel of the foot. Legrange may have invented the traditional roller skate, but it was Plimpton who perfected it.

When Plimpton's skates first caught on in the United States, skating was only for rich people. Roller rinks were expensive and it was hard to become a member. The people who went to the rinks got all dressed up—the men in suits and the women in their long fancy dresses and matching hats. They called it "rinking."

Roller skating was a lot tougher back then. The wheels didn't roll easily. Skaters really had to push themselves to get started. And they certainly couldn't do any jumps or tricks. All they could do was roll around the rink again and again.

In 1880, a man named Samuel Winslow decided that skating should be for everyone—not just the rich. He started selling skates to everyone who was interested.

This popularized roller skating even more.

But the real change in the sport came a few years later when the ball bearing was invented. Ball bearings are steel balls used in all kinds of machines. When small ball bearings were placed inside the core of skate wheels, they helped the wheels to roll more freely. Now it was easier to get skates started and easier to keep them rolling. Ball bearings took a lot of the work out of skating and made it a lot more fun, and skates today—both traditional and in-line—still use them!

Suddenly roller skates were hot! People played roller games and roller-danced on their skates. Hundreds of rinks opened across the United States. Athletes began to skate. Roller polo (today known as roller hockey) leagues sprang up around the country. Skate companies sponsored races for speed skaters. People loved to watch the speed skaters zip by in their racing uniforms. The men wore tight-fitting tops, shorts, and pants. The women wore bloomers—big, baggy, long shorts over tights.

But by the 1920s, roller skating had begun to lose its popularity. Not for long, though!

During the Great Depression of the 1930s, roller skating zoomed up again. It was one of the only ways people could afford to go out and have fun. During this time, ice-skating star Sonja Henie appeared in movies, performing beautiful skating routines on ice. Her exciting moves helped make ice and roller skating more popular.

In 1935, a brand-new roller skating sport began. It was called Roller Derby. In Chicago a man named Leo Seltzer sold thousands of tickets each night to his Roller Derby competitions. He had twenty-five teams of two skaters each. The teams would race in a large rink in an indoor stadium. Skaters tried skating 3,000 miles around a track. Some skaters slept on cots on the side of the track as others went around and around. It was an exhausting sport for the skaters, but the audiences loved the show.

When the Great Depression ended, the Roller Derby became a sport made up of bigger teams. The four main teams were in Chicago, New York, Brooklyn, and Philadelphia. They traveled the United States skating and racing.

The Roller Derby wasn't the only big skating show to travel the country. A show called the Skating Vanities had talented skaters dressed up in glittering outfits performing song-and-dance routines on ice. Audiences loved both the Skating Vanities and the Roller Derby. And they loved going to rinks to skate.

Unfortunately, when World War II broke out, it was hard for skate manufacturers to get the metal they needed for their wheels. And by the end of the war,

America had forgotten about skating.

Skating became popular and exciting again in the 1970s when skate makers started using polyurethane wheels on skates. Polyurethane is a kind of plastic. These plastic wheels gave outdoor skaters a smooth ride for the first time.

The skating world was revolutionized again when a store owner in California put skateboard wheels on roller skates. Now skating really took off! The new wheels were softer and bouncier than ever before—and they came in bright, bold colors.

The skaters of the 1970s began doing all kinds of wild things on their skates—dancing, flipping, and jumping high into the air. All over the country, outdoor skaters put on their headphones and started dancing to the beat. In rinks, skaters by the thousands danced to disco music under glittering nightclub lights. Skating fever was sweeping the country!

But the popularity of roller-dancing didn't last long because people got tired of disco music. And in the 1980s, thousands of people tossed their skates into the back of their closets when jogging became the hot new exercise fad.

Today in the nineties, skating fever is sweeping the country again. Thanks to Scott and Brennan Olson, roller skating has been changed forever.

THE IN-LINE CONNECTION 3

Scott Olson of Minnesota had always loved skating. In fact, he loved ice skating so much that he became a minor-league hockey player.

Scott really missed ice skating during the summer. And he worried when he couldn't practice the sport. Then one day, Scott found something unusual in a sporting goods store. It was a roller skate with the wheels lined up in a single row.

Seeing this skate gave Scott a few ideas. He'd been looking for a way to stay in shape during the warm weather for a long time. He thought the wheels-in-a-row skates would do the trick. "When I got turned on to these skates, it was like a dream come true," Scott says. "It was just like ice skating. It was the middle of summertime and I was skating down the street with them."

Scott thought the skates would be perfect for all his hockey player friends. But first, the skate needed some improvements. It had thin wheels with only one bearing in each wheel so it wore out very quickly, and the frame came in only one size.

He contacted the California company that was making the in-line skates and found that the people who owned the company didn't have plans to improve their skate. So Scott decided to make his own version of the in-line skate. He bought a patent from a skate company that had been making in-lines for years.

To make his skate work better and last longer, Scott added another bearing in each wheel, wider wheels, and a frame that could be adjusted to fit different sizes.

Scott's brother Brennan, a high school hockey player, joined him. They began putting skates together and looking for ways to continue to improve the skate. In 1980, Scott and Brennan opened a shop in their parents' garage. Their other brothers also helped with the business.

At first, they sold their skates (which did not include a boot yet) out of a van. They only sold the skates to hockey players who would attach the skates to the bottom of their hockey skate boots. The athletes fell in love with this fun new way to train. They thought skating on in-lines would help them to improve their hockey game. "I gave them a five-day money-back guarantee," Scott recalls. "We never had anybody return them."

Later, they designed a boot that would give skaters extra ankle support. Soon other athletes, such as cross-country and downhill skiers, also started to ask for what Scott called the Ultimate Street Skate (eventually, it was renamed the Rollerblade skate) for cross-training.

After a while, people in some northern cities started to notice the in-lines. Many of these people weren't athletes. They just thought the skates looked like fun. So, in 1981, Rollerblade started sending out vans full of skates to cities such as Minneapolis and Boston. Top skaters drove these vans, showed people how to use in-line skates, and let them try out the skates.

Scott left Rollerblade in 1984 to start his own company, Innovative Sports Systems, which now makes a new kind of in-line skate that switches from wheels to an ice blade. Brennan stayed at Rollerblade and continued to develop ways to improve in-line skates. One of these improvements was to move the brake from the toe to the heel because the heel brake worked better and improved the safety of in-lines.

In 1987, Rollerblade came up with the Lightning® model. It was the first in-line skate with a lightweight nylon frame. The Lightning® weighed one pound less than all other in-line skates available on the market. Rollerblade also came up with BladeRunner®, a special model for kids and adult recreational skaters.

By this time, in-line skating had begun to spread across the United States. People in California, especially along the beachfront, enjoyed the hot new sport. Soon people in New York and other states began to take to the parks with their in-line skates. Skate sales zoomed!

In 1988, Rollerblade gathered together the most talented in-line skaters it could find to tour the country and show people their skating tricks. Known as Team Rollerblade®, these top skaters can do things like jump over cars and flip on their in-lines. Each year Rollerblade attracts thousands of people to participate in its in-line skating races. Today, dozens of in-line races are held each year. In 1989, Rollerblade hired some of the fastest in-line racers around and formed the Team Rollerblade Race Team®.

Also in 1989, Rollerblade rolled out the first skate to close with buckles instead of laces. It's called the Macroblade®. That skate was followed by Racerblade™, a skate with five wheels. Rollerblade says it's the fastest skate available.

Today, many companies make in-line skates. They include Scott Olson's company, Innovative Sport

Systems; Bauer; First Team Sports (Ultra-Wheels); Riedell; and Zanstra.

Today, one million in-line skaters are rolling all over the country—and in Europe. In fact, racing on in-line skates is so popular in Holland that people line the streets when skaters whiz by on their five-wheeled skates! Professional athletes, from members of the U.S. Speed Skating Team to members of the U.S. Ski Team, use in-lines for cross-training. These competitors believe that in-lines help them get stronger for their own sport.

And Rollerblade keeps on improving their in-lines. Some new models will have vents in the boot. These vents make the skate fit better, feel lighter, and help keep skaters' feet cool while they're on the move.

Experts expect to see more skates made especially for kids and women. "There will be more skates available at lower prices for younger kids," says John Egart of First Team Sports. "There will also be more sophisticated skates at higher prices—with faster wheels, ball bearings, and performance." His company, which makes Ultra-Wheels, already makes skates that are small enough for three-year-old kids!

Bob Harr, an engineer at Kryptonics in Boulder, Colorado, thinks the polyurethane skate wheels will become really exciting in 1991. And he should know. Kryptonics makes the wheels for many in-line skates.

Do you like to race on your skates? Or are you a skate dancer? Whatever your favorite skating activity is, you'll be able to find wheels that are just right for you, Bob promises.

And wheels will be taller, better-looking, and might even have unusual shapes built into their middles. "They will look like fancy wheels on cars," Bob says. And since Kryptonics is working on new formulas of polyurethane, the new wheels will also last longer, be bouncier, and slide less.

Will more people get on a roll in the future? Absolutely, say some experts. "I've heard that in-line skating is the single biggest thing ever to hit the sporting goods market. And I believe that," says Scott Narins, one of the owners of the Blades West and Blades East in-line skate stores in New York City. "It's a new means of transportation, it's social, it's a lot of fun."

GETTING EQUIPPED 4

Are you ready to check out some in-line skates for yourself? Skater Halsey Chait, twelve, who lives in New York City, really loves his in-lines.

Halsey, a race winner who can perform all kinds of tricks on his in-lines, started on roller skates. "I've seen a lot of people buy in-lines because they're in and then not use them at all," Halsey says. "First, kids might want to just rent them...then if they really like skating, they can go out and get in-lines."

After all, in-line skating can be pretty expensive. Skates start at about $90 a pair. Racing skates can cost more than $300. And the safety equipment can add another $60 to $125 to your costs.

Once you're sure you're going to stick with in-line skating, though, having your own pair can be fun. But before you buy, here's what you need to know in order to shop smart:

The Parts

Your in-line skates look really high-tech, right? Well, they certainly are made of some of the most modern materials. But actually your skates don't have a lot of complicated parts.

First is the shoelike part of the in-line skate, called the *boot*, or sometimes called the *outer shell*. The boot is hard and rigid and usually made of molded polyurethane plastic. It has either laces or buckles, just like a ski boot.

Inside most in-line skate boots is a removable, soft, and padded *inner boot*, or *liner*. When the inner boots get sweaty, you can pull them out and let them air-dry. You can even wash the inner boot with a mild soap. Some skates also come with a *footbed*, a part that goes inside the inner boot to help the boot fit better and prevent blisters.

Next comes the *frame*, or *chassis*. The skate boot is attached to the top of the strong, lightweight frame, and the skate wheels are attached to the bottom. At first, frames were made of steel; today, they're also made of nylon or aluminum. They come in different lengths—there are three-wheel frames for most kid-size feet, four-wheel frames for teenage and grown-up skaters, and five-wheel frames for racers.

On the frame there are *bolts* and *frame spacers* to help hold the wheels on and in place. The *wheels* are of course a very important part of the skates. Like boots, most wheels are made of polyurethane. These are the things you need to know about your wheels:

• **Durometer:** This means hardness. The higher the durometer, the harder the wheels. Softer wheels are more comfortable and help the skater to glide over bumps more smoothly.

• **Rebound:** This has to do with how much the wheels will bounce back. All wheels get a little squished against the ground every time a skater pushes off. A high rebound means wheels will bounce back fast and strong. High rebound helps skaters get more motion out of the energy they put into their skating. It also makes the wheels turn faster.

• **Diameter:** This is the size of the wheels from top to bottom. Bigger wheels go faster and last longer. Racing wheels are usually taller than other skate wheels.

• **Cores:** These are also referred to as *hubs*. The core is a hard plastic piece inside the inner wheel. Wheels with cores go faster than wheels without cores because they help retain the shape of the wheels while in use.

• **Ball Bearings:** These tiny steel balls help the wheels to spin and to keep moving. Some bearings help the wheels move faster. Semiprecision and full-precision bearings are the best and the most expensive. Non-precision bearings are usually found in lower-priced skates. Find out what kind of bearings are in the skates you're thinking of buying.

• **Axle:** The axle is the bolt that goes through the wheels and the bearings and out the other side of the skate frame. Always make sure that the nuts on the axles tighten up, and your wheels feel steady.

• **Brake:** On the outside of the boot, at the heel, is the brake made of hard rubber. Many in-line skates have a brake on only one boot, but some have a brake on both.

Wheels on the frame can either be level or "rockered." When the wheels are level, all of them touch the ground at the same time. That's good for most kinds of skating. When the wheels are rockered, the front and back wheels are a little higher off the ground than the middle wheels. Some skaters like to rocker their wheels for roller hockey, figure skating, or doing tricks. Not all in-line skates can be rockered.

The Right Skate For You

Your feet are a different size and shape than your best friend's. And you may not like to do the same things on your skates as your brother does. Well, that's why it's so important to make sure the skates you're thinking about getting are the right ones for your size and ability. Here's some advice from Scott Narins and

Jeff Kabat of Blades West and Blades East.

"The more comfortable you are, the more you're going to enjoy skating," says Scott. "And the more you enjoy it, the better you're going to get." So go for comfort first when trying on in-line skates. Your skates should fit well with just one pair of athletic socks. You shouldn't wear more than one pair of socks. Your foot really needs to know how the skate is moving.

When laced up or buckled, the boot should feel snug but not tight or uncomfortable. Jeff and Scott say it's not a good idea to buy in-line skates that are a little big so that you can grow into them. You're better off getting a less expensive pair that fits you right away.

Have the salesperson show you how to lace up or buckle the skates. Then stand up and bend your knees. Your foot should feel as if it has a lot of support. The ankles shouldn't feel wobbly. Jeff says it's OK for your big toe to touch the front of the inner boot. But your toes shouldn't feel as if they're jammed up into the front of the inner boot. And your big toe shouldn't bump up against the inside of the outer shell. Remember, these plastic shells won't stretch at all.

Some boots are made so that they can take a few different sizes of inner boot. This means you can keep buying new inner boots as your feet grow. Ask about these at the store.

Are you comfortable? If so, it's time to start checking out your skate's features. If you've never gone in-line skating before, stick with a style that's made for recreational skating. These will be a little slower than skates made for performance or racing.

Whatever kind of skating you plan to do, get a boot that is firm and supportive. The shell should feel hard and strong—almost like a ski boot. Look at the inner boot. Does it fit inside the outer shell without crinkling up? Does it feel right on your foot? If you're looking at lace-up skates, check the holes that the laces go through. These should look and feel strong. After all, you'll be pulling hard on those laces to get your skates nice and tight.

You should also test the frame. It's best to get a rigid frame for a stable ride. To test the frame, turn the skate over so that the wheels are facing you. Cradle the boot between your legs and try to twist the frame. If the frame twists, your ride will be unstable.

Examine the whole boot. Make sure nothing wiggles or rattles that isn't supposed to. Shake the skate. Do you hear any strange noises?

Next, check out the wheels. This is really, really important. Read the brochure that comes with the skates to find out about the hardness, rebound, and size of your wheels. Talk to the salesperson about the kind of skating you think you'll be doing. Remember, wheels come in different sizes and hardnesses for people of different sizes and abilities.

Bob Harr of Kryptonics says more and more wheels are being made for specific kinds of skating. Are you a racer, a roller hockey player, or just ready to have fun doing your own thing on your in-line skates? Here's what Bob recommends:

• **For racing:** Lighter, larger-diameter wheels. The higher the rebound, the better. That's because racers can use all the energy their wheels help them save. Look for wheels with a large, open cores. These cores help to get rid of some of the heat that builds up in the wheels during a race.

• **For roller hockey:** Round, soft wheels with a smaller diameter, about 70 millimeters.

• **For recreational skating:** A 78–82 durometer (hardness) is good for most skating and slightly harder wheels are used when skaters want to avoid building up heat on the wheels quickly.

• **For figure skating and slalom:** Same as above. Also, these activities call for a narrower wheel.

• **For ramp tricks:** In-line skaters who do skateboard-style tricks on a ramp should use soft wheels with high rebound. This will give them a lot of speed. Also, small wheels are best—with a diameter of about 70 millimeters.

And keep this in mind—you can always upgrade your skates. So if you're a beginning skater, you may want to start out with slow wheels and bearings and then switch to faster wheels and bearings as your skating improves.

The Safety Stuff

Don't buy those skates yet! First you've got to grab the right kind of safety gear. You can really take some nasty tumbles on your in-line skates. All the experts say that safety equipment is a must. Here's what you should use—all the time:

• **Wrist guards:** This is probably the most important piece of safety gear a skater can wear. As Jeff Kabat says, "When you fall, you always put your hands out to break your fall. And you can break your wrist if you fall on it." Wrist guards wrap around your hands and wrists. They can prevent most wrist injuries. They'll also give you more confidence because you'll know you're protected. Cost: about $25 to $30.
• **Knee pads:** A lot of skaters make four-point landings! That means they fall right on their hands and knees!

27

Knee pads can prevent banged-up, bruised-up knees. Racers and ramp skaters use large, heavy-duty pads like the ones skateboarders wear. Cost: $15 to $100.

- **Elbow guards:** These are especially important if you're trying to learn new tricks. Elbow guards are also great just in case you happen to fall backward. They're usually made of nylon and plastic. Heavy-duty pads are used by racers and ramp skaters. Cost: $15 to $100.

- **Helmets:** Your hard-shell bicycle or skateboarding helmet can do double duty as a skating helmet. As in-line skating champion Eddy Matzger says, "You only have one head. Protect it." Cost: $30 to $50.

- **Gloves:** These protect hands from scrapes and bruises. Because you're already wearing wrist guards, gloves are optional, but definitely not a bad idea.

Skate Maintenance

Once you've got your in-line skates, you've got to keep them in top condition. Otherwise you won't skate as well. And skate maintenance is simple, so don't forget to ask your salesperson about it.

Rotate your wheels every 50 miles or when you start to notice that your wheels are wearing down. How can you tell when it's time to rotate? Hold your skates up, with the front of the skate facing you. Are the inside edges of your front wheels more worn down than the outside edges? If so, switch! Take the wheels on your left skate and move them to your right skate. And move the wheels on your right skate to your left skate. Also, turn the wheels so that the side that was facing in is now facing out. If this seems confusing, just remember this: the edge that is worn should face out.

The booklet that comes with your skates should tell you how to make the switch. Some skates even come with little wrenches for removing the wheels. If yours don't come with a wrench, ask the salesperson what kind of tool to use.

When you are rotating the wheels, clean the bearings with a dry cloth (never use a wet cloth) to keep them free of grime and dust. This will help your bearings to last longer. You must also make sure that nuts and bolts (axles) go back on nice and tight.

If your wheels get wet, skate around a little and let them air-dry. Then with a dry cloth or tissue, dry the wheels completely. Scott Narins suggests taking the bearings out and wiping them off with a towel. Keep the outer boots looking clean and sharp with a vinyl protector or wipe them with a damp cloth.

Eventually your wheels and bearings will wear out. In-line skate makers expect that in-line skaters will have to replace wheels after about 500 to 1,000 miles of skating, depending on the kind of wheels you purchase.

But if you notice that your wheels are really wearing down, take your skates to a store and get some advice.

You can replace your wheels with a new set from Kryptonics, Hyper, Labeda, Sims, or other manufacturers. Look at the durometer, rebound, and size and think about what kind of skating you might do in the next 1,000 miles. You can expect to pay about $40 to $100 for a set of eight new wheels.

How can you tell when it's time to replace your bearings? When the bearings start to make a lot of noise and the wheels stop turning smoothly. If one skate starts to drag a little, you'll know that the bearing in that skate is worn out. You should be able to buy a complete set of new bearings at any in-line skate shop for about $30 to $35. Some bearings cost as much as $70 per set.

You can count on brakes wearing out after a while, too. Keep checking your brakes to see if they're wearing down. You'll know it's past time to change brakes if you hear any kind of scraping sound when you brake. You can buy replacement brakes at the skate store for about $3 each.

Once you have all your equipment together, you might want to modify your in-lines a little. If you're buying new wheels, check out some new colors. You might even want to mix and match. "Some kids will put four different colors on each axle," says Bauer's Nate Otis. "I also see a lot of sticker action on the skates."

Some people are actually drilling holes into their skates for ventilation. Others may add a power strap around their ankle. The power strap is a Velcro strap that helps to close the boot even tighter around the ankle. Ray Hamel of Hamel's Action Sports in Mission Beach, California, says he customizes a lot of in-line skates. "Sometimes we add a ski boot buckle or a toe stop."

When it comes to skating style, wild, bright, and comfortable is at the top of the fashion hit list. In-line skaters in California love to roll along in swimsuits and bright neon colors. East Coasters go for bike shorts or shiny tights, and bright T-shirts. In the Midwest during the colder months, a lot of skaters like to layer up with sweatpants and sweatshirts. And everywhere, skaters know that fanny packs are a great place to stash extra gear.

Now that you know how to get equipped, you're ready to learn how to use your skates. So, flip the page!

GET ROLLING! 5

OK, you've got your skates, you're wearing all your safety gear—you're ready to roll!

But before you put those skates on, you've got to make sure everything is shipshape. Check the axles and the wheels to make sure everything is tightened up. Make sure the wheels feel steady and the nuts on the axles are good and tight. If you're not using new skates, you should also examine your brakes. Make sure they're not too worn, that the metal bolt isn't showing through the rubber. If it is, change the brakes.

Is all your equipment in order? Are you geared up for safety? If the answers are yes, then it's time to take a few tips from the experts:

• **Weight a minute:** Learn the difference between in-line skates and roller skates. On regular roller skates, you try to balance your weight evenly between your right and left feet. On in-line skates, you have to shift your weight from side to side. Learning how to make that shift is really important.

• **The wet set:** Don't skate over water or oil. These make you trip very quickly—and harm your skates! If you do skate through something wet, just go straight through without turning. Then give your wheels a chance to dry off before pushing off hard or turning sharply.

• **Ground it!** Stick with pavement that is dry, flat, and clear of sand, gravel, and leaves. Not only is this safer, but it will help wheels and bearings last longer.

• **Get light:** Don't skate at night unless there is proper lighting. Otherwise you could end up tripping over bumps that you can't even see!

• **No parking zone:** Stay away from traffic. Don't skate in the street—or in any crowded area. Obey all traffic laws. Be courteous to other athletes. When passing others, always give a warning and pass on the left.

• **Nice and easy:** Skate under control at all times. Some of the wheels on in-line skates are superfast.

• **Your turn:** Learning to turn will help you control your direction and speed.

• **Watch out below:** Don't head for the hills. In-line skates pick up speed on even the smallest hills. Stay on level ground.

- **Stop that:** Make sure you learn how to stop rolling before you go anywhere.
- **Be bright:** Wear bright, bold clothing. Not only will you look great, but everyone will be able to see for your own safety!
- **Sensaround:** Don't skate with earphones. You need to hear what's going on around you. Plus, the music can interfere with your concentration.

Got that? OK, it's time to boot up. Head for a nice, quiet place—inside your house or in your yard. Carpeted rooms and yards are good places to lace up for the first time to get used to the balance—and you won't go rolling away on carpeting or grass.

Now lace or buckle your skates up tightly around your ankles and at the top of the boots. This will give you extra support, and your ankles won't wobble when you stand!

Stand still, bend your knees, then try shifting your weight from side to side or standing on one foot at a time. Try walking around a little on the carpeting or grass just to get used to the feeling of being on wheels. Spend some time just moving around until you feel comfortable on the skates.

Then head for the smoothest, flattest, most level surface you can find. Empty parking lots are good places to start off. You may want to bring a friend along to help you out.

The first thing to know is that in-line skates don't work like traditional roller skates. So just follow these suggestions:

• Bend your knees. Bent knees are important because when your knees are bent, your weight is directly over your skates. This gives you better control and keeps you in balance.

• Angle your right foot out a little (as in a two o'clock position).

• Push off with your right foot by moving it far out to the side.

• Your left foot is gliding. The foot that glides carries the weight and gives you the stability you need.

• Keep your hands low and in front of you—uncontrolled arms will throw you off balance.

• Now bring your right foot up to meet with your left foot.

• Push off in exactly the same way with your left foot as you did with the right.

• Now shift your weight over to the right foot.

• Concentrate on each stride, on shifting your weight and keeping your knees bent, and soon you'll be gliding comfortably.

Think about balancing on each foot as you go.

Once you're experienced, you'll be able to balance completely on one foot or the other. You'll probably bend your knees and upper body a lot more, too. You should really get into a crouch—almost as if you're getting ready to sit down. And that will give you the power to push off harder. If you feel as if you're losing your balance, just crouch a little lower.

You can use your arms for balance or sprinting. Swing them back and forth gently at first, not side to side. Later, when you want to get a burst of speed, swing them more strongly. How can you tell when you're swinging your arms the right way? Take a tip from champion Eddy Matzger: "When I'm swinging my arms, I bring my hand up and touch my nose lightly after each stroke." When racers are going for distance, they often keep their hands behind their back, but this requires more balance. Eliminating arm swinging saves energy.

Stop!

Before you head away from home with your in-lines, you have to know how to stop. The moves for basic braking are simple, but they do take some practice. Here's what to do:

- Bend your left knee.
- Begin pushing your right leg out in front of you.

• Push your right toe up so that the heel brake starts connecting with the ground.

• Bend your body forward and push down on the brake gently.

You might want to keep your knees together during braking for better balance.

NOTE: If both your skates have brakes, you can choose which foot you wish to brake with.

Turn!

The simple way? As you're rolling, put your knees together and lean in the direction in which you want to go.

Skilled skaters sometimes do an in-line turn. Here's how it goes: Put one foot slightly behind the other. Lean in the direction in which you want to go. That means for a right turn, you would put your right foot in front and lean right. For a left turn, put your left foot in front and lean left.

Trick Tips

Even simple tricks require practice and control. Here are some fun tricks that you can learn once you know how to push off, glide, and stop. *Always wear your safety gear.*

Jumps: Find something simple to jump over. A crack in the sidewalk is a good starter because you can land on it without tripping. Think about getting your whole body over the crack, not just your skates. Build up your speed so you can jump easily. About five feet in front of the crack, get ready to jump. Now lift off with *both* feet together. Land with one foot in front of the other and be ready to glide. With practice you will gradually jump over bigger objects!

The curb roll: Pick a nice, low curb for your first few tries at this trick. Do this only in an area that has no traffic. Go slowly and look at your landing point as you approach the curb. Coast right off the curb. As you land, bend your knees. That way, your knees will absorb the shock. You may want to keep your hands out in front of you for balance.

The toe-heel glide-along: Start out by skating slowly. Position one foot slightly in front of the other. Lift the heel of your back foot so you're on the front wheel of that skate. Lift the toe of your front foot so you're on the back wheel of the other skate. Glide as long as you can while using your arms to keep yourself balanced.

Once you've tackled these tricks and you want to learn more, you can call up Rollerblade In-Line Skate

Association (RISA) at (800)255–RISA.

In-Line Activities

The nice thing about in-line skating is that you can do so many different fun things on skates—tricks, dancing, racing, hockey, or just plain gliding along. Here's the scoop!

Roller hockey: People have been playing hockey on the ice for hundreds of years. They've also played the game on traditional roller skates. But in-line skates are more like ice skates, so a lot of street hockey players are going for in-lines. Before you play roller hockey on in-line skates, you need to develop a few special skills. According to Tom Peffer of Culver City, California, you should be able to skate backward, stop quickly, and turn. And he should know! After all, he runs the 175-member Rollerblade Los Angeles Rollerhockey League.

Tom and other experts say that roller hockey also requires a lot of protective gear. What's important? A helmet, elbow pads, hockey gloves, shin pads, and a face mask.

Racing: A lot of speed skaters are heading for in-lines. "You are more stable in motion—there is less chance of falling with the wheels in a row," said Henry Zuver of the National Outdoor Marathon Roller Skating Association as he compared in-lines to traditional roller skates. "And you can travel further with one stride. Athlete to athlete, I can go faster further on in-lines." Henry says that for a marathon race, you'll start picking up speed once you can skate for four hours without stopping to rest!

If you want to train for racing, whether it be for a marathon or a sprint race, you need to be able to control your skates extremely well. Racing is really only for very skilled skaters—and skaters who are willing to put in a lot of time. You'll need to spend hours each week just skating and building up speed and endurance.

Streetstyle: Doing dance moves on your in-lines is a little trickier than dancing on roller skates. But it can be done. If you're dancing with somebody else, make sure the lead person is a half step behind the other skater. Then bend your knees, put your heels close together, and glide! You can also dance by yourself. Just practice gliding and turning, and you're sure to come up with some snazzy steps. Some top skaters can do all kinds of figure skating moves.

Ramp riding and stunt skating: These are basically the same kinds of tricks that skateboarders love doing—fast, daring, and scary. Doing tricks on half-pipes or just around town is only for extremely advanced skaters. You really need the skills of an acrobat to do flips, splits, and wall rides. If you're going to try this kind of stuff on your in-lines, get training from an in-line skate shop professional. And make sure you wear your safety gear!

CROSS-TRAINING

It's hard to believe any sport that's so much fun could be good for you, but in-line skating is a terrific fitness-builder. A lot of professional athletes cross-train with in-line skates, including members of the National Hockey League, the U.S. Ski Team, and the U.S. Ice Speed Skating Team.

Patrick Karns, an athletic trainer at St. Cloud State University in St. Cloud, Minnesota, studied skaters who rolled around a track for forty-five minutes three times a week. He watched their progress over eight weeks and found that the in-line skating helped the skaters build their aerobic strength. "It's a good fitness tool," he says. "All too often, people have to either go biking or running. This is in between—you can cover a lot of ground and you get the thrill of speed, but you also work out your muscles. And we found out that you can get in better shape and reduce body fat."

"If people take precautions, they're a good cross-training device," says John Atkins, the director of conditioning for the U.S. Ski Team. "They are fun, they are a great workout. But people have to be really careful about where they skate—not with the cars."

The best way to work out on in-lines, John says, is to skate up a small hill. "Find some gentle hills and do some nice uphill sprints," he says. This will give you a workout that's a lot like doing an uphill sprint on a bicycle. But of course, uphill sprints are only for experienced skaters.

Team Rollerblade member Chris Morris "catching big air"!

Team Rollerblade racers Bruce Jackson (left) and Chris Morris (right) ripping along the California beachfront.

**Superdynamic Team Rollerblade member Jill Schulz
with Dalmatian friend.**

**Lacing up! Make sure those laces are tight and secure
before rolling. And don't forget the knee pads!**

Junior Team Rollerblade members make sure their knees stay bent for extra balance and power! Junior Team Rollerblade is the youth division of Team Rollerblade.

You can definitely get anywhere faster on your in-lines and it's a lot more fun too!

People have been playing roller hockey (also called roller skate hockey) for hundreds of years!

Today in-line skates have made roller hockey a hot new sport!

This contraption called the pedo-motor was used to "accelerate the motion of walking" but was also considered a cure for flat feet!

Rock 'em, sock 'em action—that's the Roller Derby! In the 1930s and 1940s, teams would travel across the United States skating and racing for roaring crowds.

49

The pedespeed, like the pedomotor, was another short-lived invention. But in the 1870s some people enjoyed them anyway!

Wouldn't you rather be skating today?

AMAZING SKATERS 6

Every in-line skater is pretty amazing. But here are a few who really dazzle!

JILL SCHULZ

Jill Schulz has worked pretty hard at fitness all her life, and she works really hard as a member of Team Rollerblade. Jill, who's been in-line skating for more than four years, skates with the team and helps make up daring dance routines for the skaters.

Jill, whose father is "Peanuts" cartoonist Charles Schulz, grew up in northern California, riding and training horses and ice skating. When Jill was ten, she started entering ice skating competitions. Sometimes she'd have to get up for practice at four-thirty in the morning!

Later Jill went on to skate in such professional skating shows as the Ice Follies. She also started roller skating. She discovered in-line skates one day while skating near the beach. But she didn't really get on an in-line roll for another year and a half. Then she moved quickly, learning dance routines and tricks and teaching other people how to use in-lines.

Today, Jill skates for at least an hour every day. She spends hours making up new dance steps, teaching, and rehearsing. Jill and the team members perform their wild dance routines all over the country—and around the world!

Besides dancing, Jill loves to do stunts on her in-line skates. "I skate on the half-pipe, go off a 4-foot launch ramp, and I can jump off about eight stairs," she reports. "But the three tricks that are my favorite are a series of cartwheels into a one-handed cartwheel, a cantilever [a spread eagle where you sit real low and lean way back], and an axle—that's where you take off on your right foot, do one and a half turns in the air, and land backwards—on your left foot!" Skateboarders call that stunt a 540.

What's the most amazing stunt this daredevil skater has ever done? Once she jumped off a flight of ten stairs. Can you imagine the size of the leap? "We were making a commercial and somebody else jumped off the stairs," Jill says. "So I told the director I could do that. I'd never jumped that far before. But I did it!"

It sounds like Jill can do just about anything she works at. She's even got her whole family—including her dad—on a roll!

DAVID G. MILES, JR.

David G. Miles, Jr., of San Francisco, California, cares a lot about kids and roller skating. He believes that skating is a great way for kids to have fun. So he spends a lot of his free time showing them tricks.

David is the president of the Outdoor Roller-skating Association of America (ORA), a group that puts together skate races. He's also the president of the Golden Gate Park Skate Patrol. He helps to keep the thousands of people who roll through the park safe and happy. His skate patrol heads out every weekend to teach skating, help skaters who are injured, and keep skate traffic moving. All the members of the patrol have to know first aid and CPR (cardiopulmonary resuscitation).

David has also gotten the patrollers to skate for charity. They've raised money for such groups as Greenpeace, the Boy Scouts, and the March of Dimes. Last year they skated from San Francisco to Los Angeles to tell people about the dangers of drugs. "Skating is very positive, a positive message to kids," David says. "They see how much fun we're having and want to do it, too."

David has been skating ever since he moved to San Francisco twelve years ago. "I used to skate as a little kid, too, with my church group," he recalls. But when I moved to California, I started skating outdoors. I haven't been to a rink more than ten times since. It's just too good skating outdoors. The sun is shining, and it's just a real good feeling."

People who know this skater say he gives them a real good feeling. He helps a lot of kids who are in trouble or who have problems at home. Maybe David knows that some kids just need a break. When he was a kid he moved eleven times! His mom was divorced five times. David also dropped out of school in the tenth grade.

Today, David works as a recreation director in San Francisco and lives with his wife, Rose, and his little girls, Melanie and Tiffany. Naturally, he skates to work!

David skates nearly every day. He uses traditional and in-line skates—and he loves them both. "I didn't think much of the in-lines at first. But now, when it comes to long-distance, it's in-lines all the way!" he says.

REMY AND HALSEY CHAIT

Remy and Halsey Chait of New York City are two of the fastest, trickiest brothers around. At least they're quick and tricky on their in-line skates! Both brothers can do all kinds of jumps and spins, and Remy even loves to dance on his in-lines.

Remy, fifteen, skated in the National Outdoor Marathon Roller Skating Association's (OMRA) biggest race, from Athens to Atlanta, Georgia. The Athens to Atlanta competition has a 40- and 85-mile race. Remy raced for 85 miles and won for his age group. He finished the race in about five and a half hours.

Remy has been roller skating for about five or six years. He's been in-line skating for about two years. He skates nearly every day during the warmer months and builds up his legs during the winter. He also plays ice hockey.

Remy's very strong, but even he got a little tired during the Athens to Atlanta race. "I thought of stopping in the middle, but then I thought about what would happen if I didn't finish, what everybody else would think. Pride kept me going." As it turned out, Remy took only one break during the whole race!

Remy's brother Halsey, twelve, started skating after seeing how much fun Remy was having. He also competed in the Athens to Atlanta race. He skated in the half-distance race and came in first in his age group for in-line skaters.

Although Halsey has only been skating for two

years—and on in-lines for only one year—he's already built up his speed. He loves doing tricks on his in-lines—skating the slalom course in Central Park, riding on walls, doing jumps, and skating on ramps. He also loves jumping long distances.

What's next for these talented brothers? Remy hopes to someday enter some of the skating races in Holland. He'd also like to be a member of a skating team. Halsey wants to get a sponsor to help cover the costs of skating. Training, traveling, and competing get expensive.

The brothers have some advice for skaters who want to become "quick and trick." "You have to just go out and do it a lot," Remy says. "Have fun doing it. And be committed."

EDDY MATZGER

Eddy Matzger has always been athletic. For years he played tennis and volleyball, swam and ran. "Anything I could get my hands on," Eddy recalls. But then one day about three years ago, his friend Bill Le Bon got a pair of in-line skates. And once Eddy tried in-line skating, everything else seemed dull. "You just feel so free," Eddy says of in-line skating. "It's like you're flying."

This Berkeley, California, in-line skater sure does

fly on his skates. He moves so fast that he's become the 1990 in-line skating champion of the United States for 10-kilometer races and longer distances! How fast has Eddy gone? Well, he's not sure. But when he was in Mexico recently, a cyclist with a speedometer told Eddie he was skating at 54 miles per hour! And he holds the current record time for the 10-kilometer race distance—16 minutes and 59 seconds! Today, Eddy skates everywhere—shopping, to the laundromat, to classes at college. "You can go three times as fast as you can walking," he says. "You can do three times as much during the day."

Eddy also spends plenty of time keeping his speed up. He skates four or five times a week, swims, runs, and goes speed skating on ice. His favorite way to train is to follow his school's women's cycling team on their training route through the Berkeley hills. He also lifts weights twice a week. "But I don't think weight lifting is very beneficial for in-line skating," Eddy says. "I found that if I have bulky legs I feel slower."

Eddy really fell in love with in-line skating when he visited Holland with his family. "My grandmother still lives in northern Holland," he explains. "So we went there for her eightieth birthday."

Eddy and his family rented a boat and traveled from town to town. When they docked in the afternoons, Eddy would put on his in-line skates and go exploring. He found that in-line skating is very popular there. Eddy loved the speed and bought a pair of five-wheel skates made specially for racing.

Eddy dreams of returning to Holland and competing in the big races there. He's even studied the Dutch language for three years so he'll feel right at home. The people in Holland know all about Eddy and his speed. A skating company there is even making a skate called the Eddy Matzger Special!

TOM CANNON HOWARD

Tom Cannon Howard has been skating on in-lines for about ten years. But he already knew a lot about in-line skating because he has been ice skating since age four! When Tom first started on in-lines, he wanted to take a long trip. He trained by skating with a backpack filled with rocks on his back. He also wore 5-pound ankle weights. Then Tom skated from Denver to Minneapolis—a mere 950 miles!

Tom earned $5,000 for a halfway house in Colorado for making the trip. It took him nineteen days, and he camped out the whole time. He also carried a 45-pound pack on his back! "In the beginning, I could only go 2 or 3 miles at a time before stopping to rest," Tom recalls. "After a while I got stronger and could go up to

15 miles before resting."

Sometimes Tom would stop on the side of the road and use his backpack as a pillow. He'd also put a shirt over his face to protect him from the sun. When he skated, he carried a stick behind his back. He'd use the stick to help him get uphill.

The trip was very exciting, but Tom did have a few scary moments. When he was in eastern Colorado he saw a lot of copperhead snakes. He knew they were dangerous and worried that a snake might crawl into his tent. "In the morning I had to feel all around me before I got up to make sure a snake hadn't gotten in," Tom says. He also "hit the wall" from the sixth through the tenth days. When a marathon runner or skater hits the wall, it means he feels that he can't go any farther. When that happened to Tom, he was in northern Nebraska. It was very quiet and lonely. The area looked like a desert. "The cars would go by at 70 miles per hour and I would just scream at them," Tom says. "When I'd finally get to a town I'd wish I was at the next town."

After the tenth day, Tom made it through the wall and started to have fun again. He began to enjoy the countryside and all the people he met on the way. "In South Dakota I got to see how they milked the cows," Tom says. "I also had a big pancake breakfast."

Since his big skating trip, Tom has gone pretty far. In 1987, he bicycled across the country to raise money for Save the Children. That took thirty-five days. He still skates a lot and loves playing Bandy, a mixture of hockey, soccer, and golf—played on ice. Tom is a player and coach for the U.S.A. Bandy Team.

Today, Tom is proud that he has accomplished so much. He says the hardest part was believing that he could go the distance. "After going through the wall, I realized what I was accomplishing and that it was going to lead me into bigger and better things in life," Tom says. "It's great realizing that you can do whatever you set your mind to."

PAT WALL

When Pat Wall lived in Miami, Florida, he loved going in-line skating with big groups of friends. Sometimes they'd skate 50 miles in a day—just going to different parks, stores, and movie theaters.

Today, Pat lives in Minneapolis. And he can do flips, jumps, splits, and stair jumps on his in-lines. One of Pat's favorites? "I like to jump over vans," he says. "Like straight up and down. Sometimes 12 feet."

How did Pat learn to do such an amazing (and dangerous!) stunt? He practiced long and hard. He also fell down—a lot. "I took some hard bumps," Pat says.

"But that's because I was trying to do some wild stuff. I just kept trying harder and harder and getting more and more bruises."

Pat doesn't get many bruises anymore, even though he does all kinds of wild tricks. On a ramp, Pat can do foot grabs, airwalks, 360 spins, and hand plants.

Off the ramp, Pat can do all kinds of different splits. He can skate on his toes and do toe spins. He can also jump up into the air and whirl around several times. Sometimes he even does wall rides, where skaters actually kick their feet up on the wall and skate the wall! Pat's favorite off-ramp trick is a hand flip. To do that, he skates along quickly, throws his hands down on the ground, and flips up into the air. "I love that because it really surprises people," he says.

Pat has unusual plans for the future: He wants to go to Australia and help teach people about in-line skating. He's also a photographer and dreams of doing nature photography. "Both things sort of tie together for me," Pat says. "My friends and I are into having a great time on our in-line skates, doing anything from dancing to traveling to doing tricks."

BILL LE BON
Some folks just like to be on the move, and skater Bill Le Bon is one of them. He likes moving on his in-

lines so much that he skated clear across the country!

Bill skated out of San Francisco on his trek in May 1990 and arrived in Washington, D.C., in September— 134 days later!

When Bill first got his in-line skates, he didn't know what to do with them. "I went down a hill, lost control, had a crash—and I felt stupid," he recalls. "I didn't know how to stop on them." After pal Eddy Matzger began zipping around town on the skates, Bill decided to give in-lines another chance. Now he loves in-line skating!

Bill decided to take his big skating trip for a couple of reasons. He really wanted to see the country. And he wanted to do something to help the environment. He dreamed of a cross-country road just for bikers, skaters, walkers, horses, and wind- and solar-powered cars. Bill found out about a group that was walking across the United States to teach people about pollution. It was a perfect opportunity!

Bill was sad to find out that he had already missed the beginning of the trip. He thought he'd be able to catch up with the group if he traveled on his in-lines. But once Bill got on his skates two weeks later, he just kept going!

Bill camped out all along the way. He kept his food and clothing in a baby jogger, a three-wheel baby stroller with a special cover and brakes. Bill pushed the jogging stroller along in front of him as he skated.

Since no nationwide bike or skating path exists, Bill had to travel by road. He tried to stick with smaller roads, but he did skate along the sides of some four-lane highways. And that wasn't always fun. "I had a great trip. I had a really good time," Bill says. "But dealing with traffic was just the worst part."

Bill skated through Sacramento, Reno, Salt Lake City, Denver, Omaha, Des Moines, Chicago, Toledo, South Bend, Gary, Cleveland, Akron, Youngstown, Pittsburgh, and Washington, D.C. "I wanted to connect with as many big cities as I could," Bill says. "Because that's where the problems are with transportation—all the cars and the traffic jams. And also that's where I could get seen more and get my message out. Also, cities are where most skaters hang out."

Bill has a lot of great memories of his unusual trip. "The high point was the High Point—the highest continuous road in the United States. I was crossing the continental divide and going over Rocky Mountain National Park, at 12,200 feet," Bill says. "Incredible scenery...."

Unfortunately, Bill also had some bad times on the trip. In Nevada, he was nearly hit by a truck. "It came into my lane and missed me by a foot," Bill says.

"I stopped there for a minute and said my prayers." Coming into Washington, D.C., was pretty scary, too. Bill got to the city during rush hour, when the streets were clogged with cars. "I just got off the road and waited for a couple of hours until the traffic died down."

Bill raised $2,500 for Rails to Trails during his trip. That's a group that takes abandoned railroad tracks and makes them into biking, skating and hiking trails. Rollerblade gave Rails to Trails another $2,500.

Now Bill's working with environmental groups and planning another long trip. He wants to skate across Europe and Asia next! He thinks a few other people will join him. Wouldn't you?

IN-LINE LINGO 7

Are you "catching air" and "shredding" on your skates with the best of them? Well, even if you're just learning how to stand on your in-line skates, you can talk in-line talk with the best of them.

Adding style: Making tricks better. When you do this, you're *styling.*

Air: A general term for any type of trick in which you leave the ground and go up into the air. Skateboarders, skiers, and snowboarders all use this expression. And you don't "get air," you "catch some air." If you go really high off the ground, you've "caught big air."

Air walk: A ramp trick. As they leap, skaters put one leg way out and the other leg far forward. It's sort of like doing a sideways split in the air.

Axle: This is when ice or in-line skaters jump up into the air and spin around one, two, or three times before they land.

Bail: A skateboarding word. In in-line skating, a skater bails when he has given up on a move and has decided to fall in a controlled way.

Bailing the laces: When California skaters customize their skates by adding a ski-boot-type buckle on the top, they stop tying their laces. They say they bailed their laces.

Carbo loading: Racing skaters and runners eat a lot of carbohydrates, usually pasta, the night before a big race. It's supposed to give them extra energy.

Catching air: See *air.*

Chopsticks: A dance movement for intermediate skaters in which they crisscross their feet while turning around in a continuous circle.

Coping: The metal rail at the very top of a ramp.

Crossover: A skating move in which one foot crosses over in front of the other. The crossover helps skaters make smooth turns and is essential for roller hockey.

Drafting: Following close behind someone else and letting them "cut the wind" for you. This means that they shield you from an opposing wind, which would otherwise make you use more energy. Bicycle racers sometimes do the same thing.

Drop in: A ramp trick. Skaters stand on the edge of the top of the ramp and just jump in. This gives them a lot of speed—enough to shoot them up the other side of the ramp.

Fakie: Any trick in which the skater lands backward. The word also means doing a trick in reverse.

Foot grab: This is just what it sounds like. When a skater is up in the air, he just grabs his foot. To really make this a styling move, the skater might want to move his foot forward, backward, or out to the side.

Freestyling: Performing dance-type moves on skates. You have to be skating long enough to have style before you can freestyle.

Grapevine: This is a lot like chopsticks, but instead of

lifting their feet off the ground to crisscross, skaters simply go up on their heels or toes. Also, this is a sideways move, not a circular one.

Grunt: Going uphill.

Half-pipe: A big U-shaped ramp. Skaters start at the bottom and work their way up to the top. The top edge is called the "lip."

Hand plant: Doing a handstand on top of a ramp before skating down.

Hockey turn: A way to slow down and stop. For experts only. Don't confuse this with a hockey stop, which you *never* do on in-line skates.

Jamming: Traveling fast. For advanced skaters only.

Kicking some asphalt: Skating hard.

Lacer: A device that can be added to skates so that you don't have to tie the laces.

Manual: Doing a wheelie on back wheels.

Ollie 180 or Ollie 360: Another word from skateboarding. The skater jumps into the air and turns halfway (180 degrees) or completely around (360 degrees) before landing.

Power carve: The skater does a parallel turn, but instead of slowing down, he gives himself more speed and power by really bearing down with his feet.

Power slide: A daring way to stop. Not for beginners.

Rail slides: Also called a 50/50. On some brands of in-lines, skaters can actually remove one of the inner wheels. This leaves enough of a gap so that skaters can slide their skates along the coping, that metal rail at the top of the ramp. This is a lot like a trick that skate-boarders do.

Raspberry: This is what skaters get when they fall and scrape the back of their legs.

Ripping: Traveling fast.

Road rash: This is what skaters get when they scrape more than just the back of their legs.

Rockering: Skilled skaters sometimes adjust their skates so that the middle wheel or wheels are a little lower than the outer wheels. This helps them turn faster and more easily.

Roller hiking: Skating on rough ground.

Roller hockey: Hockey played on in-line skates.

Scrub: When skaters fall, they say they've "taken a scrub."

Serpentine: This is when skaters do a lot of small, short, quick side steps as they move along.

Shoot it: The way advanced skaters head downhill.

Side surfing: A cool trick to do on a slalom course. The feet are turned out so that heels are together and knees are over toes. There are a few variations on this trick.

Skating goofy: On a slalom course, most skaters move along with their left foot in front. Skaters who roll through the slalom with their right foot in front are said to be "skating goofy."

Slalom: A small hill on which cones are set up and the skater skates downhill between them. You need great balance for this.

Spread eagle: A cool stunt. Skaters jump up, spread their arms and legs out wide, then bring them back together and land.

Stair surfing: For experts only! Skaters move along at medium speed and actually ride down a set of stairs. No one but a pro should try this.

Streetstyle: Stunts on half-pipes and ramps, or dance-style tricks.

Styling or Stylish: Really making a trick look good, giving it some super form and positioning in the air.

Three sixty (360): A full turn (360 degrees).

T-stop: This is when skaters drag one foot to slow down and stop.

Tweaking: Adding a lot of style. Example: Instead of jumping into the air and grabbing your foot before landing, you grab your foot and stretch it back behind you. You've "tweaked" the trick so that it's stylish.

Wall ride: Literally skating along the side of a wall. Skaters move along and kick their feet up on the wall for a short ride. Very tricky and for skilled skaters only.

Wall ride 360: A tough trick. The skater jumps off a wall and does a 360 degree spin before landing.

GROUPS, CLUBS, AND COMPETITIONS

8

Want to get on a roll with people across the country? Well, the sport is still so new that it's tough to find out where all the in-line skaters are skating, but we've got a few helpful hints.

CLUB ROLLERBLADE
Skate Association Director
5101 Shady Oak Road
Minnetonka, Minnesota
55343

The folks at Rollerblade have two different types of Club Rollerblade memberships that in-line skaters can join. You can get full details by writing to the address above or calling the special toll-free number for the Rollerblade In-Line Skate Association (RISA)™. That number is (800)255–RISA. You can get someone to answer questions at that number (they're very nice!).

If you become a **Recreation Member**, you'll receive:
- A membership card good for discounts. Most of these discounts are on Rollerblade equipment, such as knee pads, wrist guards, and wheels.
- Rollerblade merchandise.
- A subscription to RISA's official publication. This comes out every other month (it might soon be increased to every month).

If you become a **Competition Member**, here's what you'll get:
- Membership card.
- Rollerblade merchandise.
- Club Rollerblade merchandise.
- A one-year subscription to RISA's official publication.
- Discounts to participate in the Rollerblade Rollerhockey Leagues, Streetstyle Competitions, and in-line races sponsored by Rollerblade.
- A one-year medical insurance policy in case you get hurt at a Rollerblade event.
- National RISA ranking. Rollerblade takes all the results from every Rollerblade in-line race and uses a

point system to rank in-line racers. The results are published in RISA's official publication.

Rollerblade Events

Call the toll-free hotline at (800)255–RISA for information about all these events. You may also be able to get information at local in-line skate shops.

Rollerblade In-Line Races

In these competitions, racers can either run a sprint or marathon race. Prizes are awarded to winners, and no traditional skates are allowed. Nine of these races were held last year. This year Rollerblade will probably hold fifteen to twenty competitions and will pitch in at a bunch of smaller races across the United States.

Rollerblade Rollerhockey Leagues

If you want to play hockey on your in-line skates, Rollerblade will help point you toward the nearest league you can join. They may also give you advice on how to start a league or play in a tournament. Call the RISA toll-free number to find out more.

Rollerblade Streetstyle Competitions

Once these contests get going, they'll be for in-line skaters who love to do stunts off half-pipes or dance on their in-line skates. This year Rollerblade is having members of Team Rollerblade show off their streetstyle moves during in-line races. Team members are also showing people how to perform streetstyle stunts of their own.

NATIONAL OUTDOOR MARATHON ROLLER SKATING ASSOCIATION (OMRA)
Henry Zuver
P.O. Box 181
Pine Lake, Georgia 30072

This group helps put together long-distance races for in-line and traditional skaters. Their races are usually over 50 kilometers and can be as long as 150 kilometers. Last year OMRA held seven races across the United States. OMRA's biggest race is the 85-mile Athens to Atlanta race. Every competition also has a shorter race to go along with it. So the Athens to Atlanta competition also has a 40-mile race.

Last October, OMRA began having separate categories for in-line and traditional skaters. Are you interested in long-distance racing? Henry Zuver,

OMRA's director, suggests that you skate for as many hours at a time as you can while training. "It's more important to skate for four to five hours at a time than to go for 100 kilometers," he says. "The speed will come once you get to the point where you can skate for four hours without taking a break." OMRA will send you race information if you write to the address above.

SKATE EXPRESS
Kryptonics
Barry Lowe
5660 Central Avenue
Boulder, Colorado 80301

Skate Express is a newspaper put out by Kryptonics, the folks who make wheels for so many in-line skates. The newspaper comes out about four times a year and is filled with information about traditional and in-line skating. Plenty of interviews with skaters, too. You can pick up *Skate Express* at a lot of skate shops for free. If you want more information about Kryptonics products, you can write to Barry Lowe at the address above.

Kryptonics also helps to sponsor a couple of skating races. The biggest is the Tour De Malibu. Kryptonics puts on this 100-kilometer race with OMRA. The company also works with the Outdoor Rollerskating

Association (see below) on other races.

SKATER MAGAZINE
Paul A. Dunn
531 Main Street
Suite 422
El Segundo, California 90245
(213)769–6777

Skater first appeared in April of 1990. It comes out every other month and covers in-line and traditional roller skating. *Skater* seems to be up on all the news about in-lines, and articles feature interviews with top skaters and reviews of equipment. *Skater* also plans to sponsor races and other skating events, which will be advertised in the magazine. Coordinating Editor Paul Dunn says he'll be glad to answer any in-line skating questions for you if you write to him. If you want information on *Skater* races, write to the promotion manager. They're both at the address above.

OUTDOOR ROLLERSKATING ASSOCIATION OF
AMERICA (ORA)
David G. Miles, Jr., President
1855 Oak Street, #7
San Francisco, California 94117

The ORA sponsors all kinds of speed races and

competitions, from 100-meter races to freestyle dance and downhill slalom contests. Most of their competitions are in California, but they're hoping to expand. The Midget category of ORA races is open to kids between the ages of five and thirteen. Kids aged fourteen to seventeen compete in the Junior category.

When we talked with president David Miles, he said ORA was putting together a half-pipe to bring to competitions. Once that happens, ORA will have ramp-riding competitions, too.

You don't have to be a member of ORA to compete in its races. You do have to be a member to receive ORA ranking. Here's what members receive:

- Accident insurance for skaters in ORA events.
- A membership card good for a 10 percent discount at some skate shops.
- A quarterly newsletter with news about skater rankings and upcoming events.
- Discounts on hotel rooms and transportation in cities where competitions are held.

So what are you waiting for? Get on a roll!